Legacy
OF LOVE

BOOKS AND BOOKLETS BY LUCILE JOHNSON:

Enjoy Life's Journey

Mothers, Your Best Is Good Enough

Somebody Loves You

Sunny Side Up

Women of Christ: Be of Good Cheer

CASSETTES BY LUCILE JOHNSON:

The Best of Sunny Side Up

A Change of Heart

Enjoy Life's Journey

Everybody Needs Somebody

Following Divine Design

Friendships: You Can Take Them With You

The Language of Love in Marriage

Love Is the Heart of the Relationship

Mothers, Your Best Is Good Enough

On A Clear Day . . . You Can See the Real You

Somebody Loves You

Within Whispering Distance of Heaven

Women of Christ: Be of Good Cheer

Legacy
OF LOVE

Celebrating the priceless legacy
of a mother's love

LUCILE JOHNSON

WITH JOANN JOLLEY

Covenant Communications, Inc.

To the memory of my mother,
Maryann Duff Short,
whose love was—and is—my guiding star.

*I*t has been more than eighty-two years since my mother, Maryann Duff Short, held me in her arms for the very first time, her vivid blue eyes brimming with affection as she welcomed me into her world. During this extraordinary woman's lifetime, she was never a member of The Church of Jesus Christ of Latter-day Saints; she was not a wealthy woman; she never earned advanced degrees or held public office; and her most prized "career" was the nurturing of her marriage and the rearing of her children. That she did so with boundless love and grace and good humor and common sense has been the greatest blessing of my life. And though she passed from mortality when I was still a relatively young woman, never a day goes by when, for a few moments at least, I don't bask in the remembered warmth of her smile and her tender embrace. It is a price-less legacy of love, doubtless set in motion during a distant premortal life, passed down through the ages, then graciously conveyed from her generation to mine and beyond.

*E*lder Theodore M. Burton once spoke about foreordination and its importance to God's plan. His message to women of the Church was clear as he stated that "according to the plan of salvation, you were reserved or held back in the heavens as special spirit children to be born in a time and at a place where you could perform a special mission in life." He pointed out that according to the prophet Alma, individuals are "called and prepared from the foundation of the world according to the foreknowledge of God, on account of their exceeding faith and good works; . . . therefore they having chosen good, and exercising exceedingly great faith, are called with a holy calling, yea, with that holy calling which was prepared with, and according to, a preparatory redemption for such" (Alma 13:3). Elder Burton declared, "God reserved for those days some of His most valiant daughters. He held back for our day proved and trusted children who He knew, from their premortal behavior, would hear the voice of the Shepherd . . . He knew they would qualify themselves" (Conference address, *Ensign,* May 1975, 69).

More recently, Sister Margaret D. Nadauld, Young Women General President, has expressed her tender feelings on this subject. "I am inspired by the lives of good and faithful women," she observes. "From the beginning of time the Lord has placed significant trust in them. He has sent us to earth for such a time as this to perform a grand and glorious mission. The Doctrine and Covenants teaches, 'Even before they were born, they, with many others, received their first lessons in the world of spirits and were prepared to come forth in the due time of the Lord to labor in his vineyard for the salvation of the souls of men' (D&C 138:56). What a wonderful vision that gives us of our purpose on earth" (*Ensign*, Nov. 2000, 14).

My mother was one of those good and faithful women—one of the most noble human beings I have ever known. There was a deeply spiritual component to her life, and she was very close to her family in all the ways that mattered most. I recognized this great truth when, approximately a year after her passing, our oldest daughter Colleen enjoyed a marvelous experience in the Los Angeles Temple, where she had gone to do the endowment work for her grandmother.

My husband, Johnny, and I were living in Heidelberg, Germany, at the time. When we received a letter from Colleen, her first words were, "Wherever you and Dad are, please get down on your knees and pray that you can receive what I have written by the same Spirit that I have written it. Today, I have been to the Los Angeles Temple,

and I have been with Mimi (our children's name for my mother). It was so evident that Mimi was with me, that even the sisters in the temple left the seat next to me vacant, because we were surrounded by an unusual and wonderful feeling." When I read this, my heart pounded. She continued, "Mother and Dad, I want you to know that I had such a profound experience at the veil   I *knew* that Mimi was there with me, and that she had accepted the work."

Of course, joy washed over me as I read my daughter's words. But there was more! "One of the sisters said that the temple president wanted to see me," Colleen added. "I was dressed and ready to leave, and I went to speak with the president, wondering why in the world I had been summoned to his office. I was astounded when he said, 'Sister Wilson, in case you weren't aware of it, I wanted you to know that there was a beautiful and a wonderful woman with you today in the temple, and she must love you very, very much. One of her distinguishing features was that she had a head of auburn hair.'" Now, this sweet temple president was not acquainted with my daughter and had never known my mother, but what he described had been Mimi's crowning glory—her head of thick, beautiful auburn hair. There could be no doubt that she had finally accepted the gospel; and in a very tender and meaningful way, our family felt more complete than ever before.

Today, as the sweetest of memories flood my heart, I honor this remarkable woman who not only gave me life, but who gifted me with qualities of mind, body, and spirit that would enable me to embrace mortality with a fullness of joy. In sharing a few precious and memorable experiences, I express my love and admiration (and perhaps offer a bit of advice) for all mothers whose deepest desire is to rear happy, successful children.

A LOVING START

*F*rom my very earliest years, I was aware of the fact that my mother loved me without reservation or condition. If I have developed any self-confidence in my life, the person absolutely responsible for it was my mother. Somewhere in my child's mind, I knew that even though I had straight brown hair and perceived myself as rather plain, my mother thought I was beautiful, my mother thought I was brilliant, and my mother thought there was nobody in the world like me. From the very beginning, she cultivated in me a sense of being secure enough in myself to do almost anything—the assurance that I was utterly capable and talented and marvelous. Indeed, her love was so overwhelming that I truly believed she thought I walked on water. And it would be one thing if I did—but I didn't. Besides, I wasn't really all that beautiful—and I have the pictures to prove it! Still, not a bit of this was pretense on my mother's part. I knew that she truly believed I was a beautiful human being—so I believed it, too.

And she put her money where her generous, soft-spoken mouth was. I was barely five years old when I began kindergarten at our local elementary school. But Mother didn't just send me to school; she took me there herself a few days before school started, introduced me personally to the principal, and sang the praises of her pint-sized daughter! So I suppose I shouldn't have been surprised when on the very first day of school, the principal called me to her office and said, "Lucile, we have a nice little experience for you. We want you to do something for us." Smiling, she handed me a rather large piggy bank (at least it seemed large to me at the time) and five or six pennies. "Lucile," she began, "your mother said that you speak well, that you enunciate clearly, and that you can make yourself heard. So we would like you to take this piggy bank, and starting with the sixth grade, we want you to say (along with a few other lines that I've since forgotten), 'Benjamin Franklin said, "A penny saved is a penny earned."'" Then you put a penny into the bank." So there I stood, in front of the principal and the whole world—a five-year-old with absolute (though probably ill-conceived) confidence. I was ready to go!

A few minutes later I stood in front of the sixth grade, said my little piece, then declared, "A penny saved is a penny earned" while dropping a coin into the bank. It went rather well, I thought—except that I hadn't been told what to do next. So I just stood there. I could see the teacher sitting at her desk, waiting expectantly for whatever else I was to say. Long moments passed in silence, and I was beginning to feel a little bit uncomfortable.

Finally, a sixth-grade boy in the front row took matters into his own hands—he stood up and started clapping! I was utterly overwhelmed (and, I might add, instantly smitten by this older, wiser man who had suddenly become my hero). Then the rest of the sixth-graders started applauding. But I still didn't know quite what was expected of me, so I continued to stand there, doing nothing. Taking another cue (and now that I look back on it, I'm sure he must have had a little sister), this boy came over to me, picked me up, carried me to the door, stood me outside, and said with a grin, "You did good, little kid." In the meantime, the principal had apparently gotten word of my plight, as she intercepted me before I got to the next room. "When you're finished, Lucile," she said kindly, "you just repeat, 'A penny saved is a penny earned. Thank you very much.' And then you leave." With this little bit of instruction, my confidence soared, and from there on it was smooth sailing.

The memory of that experience, now nearly eighty years in the past, is as clear as if it had happened yesterday. Because my mother believed in me absolutely and trusted my blossoming talents, an elementary school principal was willing to take her at her word, and I learned that I could make my presence felt in the world—even in front of a class of sixth-graders. What a marvelous beginning to my life!

By the time I was six or seven years old, growing up in southern California's San Fernando Valley, I was ready for bigger and better things. The Adore Dairy had a beauty contest for children; it was called the "Better Baby Contest." At the time, I had straight brown hair with straight bangs in front (we called it a Buster Brown cut), and I had lost my two front teeth—not exactly beauty contest material! This was, after all, the Shirley Temple era of pretty, perky little girls with blonde, curly hair. Nevertheless, Mother took me all the way into Los Angeles on a bus to enter me into the oldest level of the "Better Baby Contest." (Even today, as I look back at the pictures, I'm just humiliated for both of us!)

Gripping my hand resolutely, Mother marched me up to the contest registration table. One of the people there said to her, "Now, you are here for what?"

My mother squared her shoulders and said, "I am entering my child in the beauty contest." I recall a fleeting image of the woman behind the table, her expression vacillating between amused and appalled. But Mother just squeezed my hand a little tighter. Only a mother would have presumed to enter a child with stick-straight hair and missing teeth along with all of those little Shirley Temple look-alikes.

"Mother," I remember saying, "are you sure?"

"Of course I'm sure," she replied without hesitation.

Now, here is the really stunning thing: I won! As I reflect back on it, all I can think of is that those judges had

to be saying to each other, "Good heavens, anyone who would bring such a child in, so presumptuous, so proud of her daughter, thinking she was such a little beauty—well, we've got to award this kid something." And they did!

I still remember the best part. Mother gave me a big squeeze, and her smile was the widest I'd ever seen as she declared, "See? I told you so!"

A few years later, a rather prestigious talent contest was being held in Van Nuys. There was going to be a big prize, so the contestants were required to register. On the spur of the moment, my mother and brother and I decided to go to Van Nuys to see the contest, which was to be presented at a theater following the evening's feature movie. I had been playing outside, my legs were dirty, and I didn't have any stockings on. I was wearing a plain little cotton dress, and slippers instead of shoes. But going anywhere with my mother was a great adventure, so I went along eagerly. When we arrived at the theater, I ran ahead and sat down in the front row, as was my habit.

After the movie, dozens of little girls in pretty costumes, their hair curled and their faces all made up, began to assemble on the stage. Soon the master of ceremonies entered and made a surprising announcement. "Due to unforeseen circumstances," he said, "we have an opening for one more contestant. Is there anybody in the audience who would like to come up and compete?"

Well, that was all I needed! I shot out of my seat and walked up on that stage—a dirty-legged, straight-haired

little urchin among all of these little girls dressed in beautiful costumes. (I do remember my mother calling out "Stop her!" from the back of the theater, but she was too late.) The emcee stared at me for a moment, then asked, "And what's going to be your talent?"

"I'm going to dance," I said.

"Is this a dance that your dancing teacher has taught you?" he inquired.

"No," I explained. "I am going to do the Charleston."

"And what kind of a dance is it?" he questioned.

"Well," I said, "I'll just make it up as I go." There was a little orchestra, and I asked if they could play "Yes, Sir, She's My Baby." They said yes, so I was on my way. I just danced my heart out, and when it was over, the audience burst into applause. After everyone had performed, they held a meter over each contestant's head to judge the level of applause; and when they got to me, the meter went wild. I took the prize! I won! Here I was, clearly the underdog, a rather plain-Jane little girl who had somehow mustered up enough chutzpah to dance the Charleston in slippers and no stockings! I believe the people were so happy for me (or perhaps so amazed) that they just clapped their hearts out. When I finally made my way to the back of the theater and into my mother's arms, she was crying. I'm still not sure whether they were tears of embarrassment or joy, but there was no doubt that she was deliriously happy for me.

Through the years, I have occasionally wondered whatever possessed me to march onto that stage in the first

place. And the answer never varies: it was because my mother had reared me to believe that I was talented, that I was beautiful, and that if I just put my whole heart into it, I could do anything! Even today, many years after her death, as I look out over audiences of two or three thousand people who have come to hear me speak, I often think to myself, "What am I doing here?" In the wake of that thought, invariably a voice whispers, "You're going to do well. Don't worry; it's going to be all right." And I think, "That's Mother. Bless her heart, Mother knows I can do it."

CONSPIRACY OF LOVE

I loved Mother for her absolute, unequivocal loyalty toward me. Feeling utterly safe with her meant knowing that she would never betray a confidence, expose me to ridicule, or embarrass me in any way. I wasn't a perfect child, and sometimes notes would come home from school saying that Lucile hadn't done some of her required work or had committed some small offense. I remember saying to Mother on one of these occasions, "Are you going to tell Dad?"

"Of course not!" she huffed, as if doing so would have been the ultimate betrayal. In reality, many mothers would have responded with, "Just wait until your father gets home!" But she and I were like cozy conspirators; I knew I could trust her with my every thought, word, and deed, and it was wonderful to feel safe and trusted in her presence. Such loyalty, I believe, is one of the greatest gifts a mother can give to her children.

As a young girl, I adored birthday parties. (I still do, if the truth be told—but that is another story altogether.)

One of them in particular was quite memorable, since it took place on a date that was definitely *not* my birthday—and it was certainly not on Mother's calendar. It seems that a few days before my birthday (I was about seven years old), I invited several of my friends to my house for a birthday party—and, of course, they all brought gifts! Naturally, Mother was totally unprepared for this, and I'm sure she was quite embarrassed. But instead of losing her temper and shooing the children away, she sent my brother out to get a store-bought cake, ice cream, and a few other little party things. I was a sensitive child, and she could have destroyed me with one look; but that wasn't Mother's way. She went right along with the party, was a fun and gracious hostess, and even handed out candy or lollipops so each one of my friends had a small favor to take home. When my brother (who was six years older than I) self-righteously insisted that I should give the gifts back, Mother said no. This was my birthday party, after all; it was just a few days early. Besides, she was so loyal to me that she would never dream of embarrassing me in front of my friends. Only later in my life, when my own children challenged me with their creative adventures, did I come to understand the true depth of her loyalty—not to mention her infinite patience, her warm and generous nature, and her incredible resilience.

Mother was not only loyal to me; I knew she believed in me and valued everything I had to say. I'll never forget the dramatic way in which this was demonstrated to me as a very young child.

It was Christmas morning—how I loved Christmas! I believed fervently in Santa Claus, and I wanted him to bring me a doll. When I had mentioned this to my father a few weeks earlier, knowing that I already had a room full of dolls upstairs, he had said, "Lucy Belle, you have so many dolls!"

"But she loves dolls," my mother broke in. "Isn't that dear!"

Now, on this Christmas morning, when I hurried downstairs to see what Santa had left, under the tree I found the most adorable doll in the whole world! She had a pink dress on, beautiful hair, a stylish bonnet, and a wonderful smile. I was overjoyed, and I could hardly believe it—a new doll, and the prettiest I had ever seen!

A little later, after the gifts had been opened and breakfast was being prepared, I took my precious doll upstairs to my room, where I had a little doll chair. I carefully put her in it, placed the doll chair on the edge of my bed, and knelt down in front of this little doll. "I want you to know," I said, my heart brimming with joy and affection, "that I love you *so much* that I will take care of you all of your life, and I will never let anything harm you." In the few seconds of silence that followed, a voice came to me. I thought it was my doll, and the voice said, "I love you *so much* that I will take care of you all of your life, and I will never let anything harm you."

Well, I grabbed that doll and ran downstairs and into the kitchen, where Mother was preparing breakfast.

"Mother, my doll is magic!" I exclaimed. "My doll is magic, and she talked to me!"

Both my father and my brother were there, and predictably, my brother wasn't exactly charmed by this announcement. "Oh, yeah," he scoffed. "A talking doll!"

My father was a bit more circumspect. "Babe," he said calmly, "are you sure you heard the doll speak to you?"

"I really did!" I insisted. Then I turned to Mother and said, "Mother, she really, really talked to me, and I heard those words!"

Without a moment's hesitation, my mother turned to the rest of the family and declared, "I know she heard those words." Looking back, I think how wise she was. She never said that my doll actually spoke, but she was insightful enough to know that somehow or other I had heard something. She had verified my reality. I have since come to believe that what I heard that special Christmas morning was perhaps my earliest spiritual experience—the whisperings of a loving Father in Heaven to an innocent child's heart. If my mother had rebuffed or discounted these fragile heavenly impulses, I might have done the same. Instead, her intuitive respect for my feelings allowed the Spirit to influence my life in wonderful ways.

THE FRAGRANCE OF MOTHER

A woman who knew my mother well once said to me, "You know, Lucile, you don't know how fortunate you are to have had your mother, because she had to be the kindest, most nonjudgmental human being I have ever known." I felt the truth of her words echo back across a lifetime of tender moments—some all but forgotten, others still vivid in my memory.

When I was about nine years old, our little rural community of Reseda, California, was rocked by a series of kidnappings. The elementary school I attended sent out stern warnings that no one but parents would be allowed to pick their children up after school, and that all students should go directly home after classes. Mother and Dad sat me down and somberly laid out the rules: I was never to accept a ride from anyone, and I was always to come straight home from school. Seeing their concern, I promised to follow their instructions to the letter.

Then came the day when one of my school friends told me there were some kittens at her house. If I could just come over, I could have a kitten. I can still see myself walking with her to her house after school; I knew I had promised Dad and Mother that I would come right home, but I thought this one time wouldn't matter. I *really* wanted a kitten! The next thing I knew, there was a car driving very slowly beside me. I looked up to see my father and my mother in that car, watching me as I walked in the opposite direction from our home.

When I got into the car, my mother was quiet and looked very distressed. My father was angry, and I knew it. They wanted an explanation, especially since they had talked to me so carefully about coming right home. I told them about the kitten. Daddy said, "Well, we came to pick you up because we were taking you out, and we were going in to North Hollywood to have dinner. But now, we're going home." That was one of the longest rides of my life.

When we got home and went inside the house, Dad said to me, "This is such a serious breach, and we were so worried about you, that you're going to have to have a spanking." He made me go and get a switch from the willow tree outside, then he gave me two or three swats on the leg. It stung a little, but worse than that, it broke my heart. I was crying as Dad walked out of the house.

Mother was sitting in her rocking chair, having observed this whole scene, and I tromped over to her, sobbing. "I just hate him," I cried. "He's so unfair!"

Her voice was sad and tender as she said, "Honey, you didn't see that your father was crying. And do you know, it

hurt him so much more than it hurt you for him to have to do this."

"I don't believe that," I murmured. But then I looked at her more closely. "Mother, you're crying."

"It just breaks my heart," she confessed. Then she said something I have remembered for more than seventy years: "Lucile, some day you'll know that to have to punish your child really does break a parent's heart." Opening her arms, she said, "Come over here and sit on my lap." I did, and she pulled my head down on her shoulder. To this day, I can still remember my feeling in her arms. She smelled like Mother—I think she used talcum powder, and she had a sweet, comfortable fragrance. Then, as my head rested against her, I felt a tear drop from her cheek onto my hair. Such a simple thing, this moment of commiseration and comfort . . . yet so typical of her tender and compassionate nature. It was vintage Mother, and I loved her for it.

Other people were often the recipients of her kindness and generosity, as well. In the floundering economy of the 1930s, we often saw homeless men—we called them hoboes in those days—in our neighborhood. Not a single soul who came to my mother's door went away empty-handed. My father would say to her, "You know Mary, everybody knows you're a soft touch. One way or another, they know." It was true; some days, there was almost a line of hapless men at our door. She would make each one a big sandwich of thick, homemade bread and fresh garden vegetables, then send them on their way with a smile and a cheery word of hope and encouragement.

One day, I noticed that someone had drawn a cat on our mailbox. It was small and roughly painted, but it was unmistakably a cat. I said nothing to Mother, but later I happened to mention it casually to one of my teachers at school. Her response stunned me. "Lucile," she said, "that is the international sign of a hobo that says 'These people are kind, and they will feed you.'" A soft touch, indeed! But Mother wouldn't have had it any other way.

MOTHER, ARE WE POOR?

I grew up during the cruel years of the Great Depression, when jobs, money, and peace of mind were at a premium. We lived in a rural area where we had a large garden and could grow much of our food, but those were real poverty days. Mother, who was educated for her day and had been a teacher before her marriage, had a sense of culture and refinement that prompted her to enroll me in both dancing and elocution lessons. Looking back on those lean times, when she would empty her small purse of nickels and dimes each week to pay for my lessons, I know that her sacrifices were great, and I can't help wondering where she tightened the strings to provide so many opportunities for me and my brother.

Despite the challenges, my mother was an expert at being cheerful—she had the original "glass-half-full" personality! Thanks to her, I grew up believing that I was not only rich, but that I lived in a beautiful home. So you can imagine the shock I felt one evening when, as a teenager, I overheard my parents talking about the fact that because of financial reverses, they might be forced to sell our home. I went to bed with a heavy, heavy heart.

The next morning, I went into the kitchen and asked the question that had kept me awake most of the night. "Mother, are we poor?"

I can see her standing in front of the sink as she threw back her shoulders and turned around to face me. "Of course not," she declared. "We're rich!" That was enough for me, and I believed it. We were rich!

I suppose she told my father about our little conversation, because a day or two later he taught me a lesson that has influenced my life all these years. One of Dad's hobbies was growing watermelons, and he grew great big, juicy, wonderful ones. On this particular morning he took me outside, and we walked among those giant watermelons, his hand gripping a large Bowie knife, my mouth watering at the thought of having a slice or two of this sweet, delectable fruit. "Lucy Belle," he said after a few minutes, "which one of these watermelons do you want?"

Of course I chose the very biggest one. I can still hear the CRACK! of his Bowie knife splitting it open, and suddenly the inside of this big, red, luscious watermelon came into view. Motioning toward it, he said, "Lucy Belle, you reach in there with your hand, and you just take the heart of that watermelon; that's the only part you have to eat. If you want another heart, we'll do another watermelon."

I was stunned. "Oh, Dad!" I exclaimed, thinking of how much fruit would be wasted.

He smiled down at me. "Lucile," he said calmly, "when you only have to eat the heart out of a watermelon, you're rich."

Years later, when I was in college, I reminded my mother of that experience. "Mother," I asked, "why did you say we were rich? We were *poor!*"

To which she replied, without a moment's hesitation, "Rich is a state of mind." And once again, her statement satisfied me; I believed it with all my heart. If rich was a state of mind, then we really *were* rich!

Recalling my "watermelon lesson" reminds me of a special friend and marvelous mother in Hawaii who once shared with me a heartwarming personal experience. She titled it "Sunshine for Breakfast."

> We had eight growing children, and it seemed like they talked about food constantly. As our six boys awoke in the morning, their eyes would open, then they would stretch and call out to me, "Mom, what's for dinner?"
>
> I had an adorable but self-employed husband. The food money was sporadic. We faithfully paid our tithing, and each morning we prayed together for the funds to feed these marvelous children.
>
> One morning, we prayed as usual. My husband left for work, and I surveyed the kitchen. No eggs. No milk. No cereal. No bread. What's for breakfast? All I found were a few carrots in the bottom drawer of the fridge. I woke the children and headed for my shower. I

locked my bedroom and bathroom doors, then I turned on the shower and knelt and cried. I asked the Lord to make those carrots nourishing and delightsome to the children. He had done it with raw meat for Lehi's children. Surely it would work for my children, too.

I blew my nose and washed my face, then turned off the shower and headed for the kitchen. Retrieving the somewhat limp carrots from the fridge, I washed and grated them coarsely and put them in my little copper-bottom sauce pan with a bit of water to steam them. As the children dressed, I announced that we had a special treat for breakfast. Back in the kitchen, I divided the steamed carrot tidbits into eight white bowls and put a dab of margarine and a sprinkle of salt and pepper in the middle of each. Then, as we prepared to say the blessing, I proclaimed, "Today, we're having sunshine for breakfast!" With a bit of hesitation they took a taste or two, then dug in

with gusto. Every tiny smidgen disappeared before they headed out for school. My son Scott was seven at the time.

On Scott's twelfth birthday, he had invited several friends to spend the night as his celebration. In a planning session for the weekend festivities, we decided we would go out for pizza and bring home videos, and the boys would spend the night on the living room floor. There would be lots of snacks and soda, cake and ice cream. Of course his brothers would be there, too. What a plan!

As I made my enormous shopping list, I asked Scott what he would like me to serve this army for breakfast. Waffles, pancakes, bacon, eggs, cereal, juice, blueberry muffins? Anything he wanted. He was very thoughtful and closed his eyes, savoring the decision. "You know, Mom," he finally said, "I remember when I was real little, and we had an awesome breakfast. I think it was the most delicious breakfast I ever had. You have probably forgotten. I think we only had it one time. We had sunshine for breakfast."

Scott was surprised to see tears in my eyes. Sometimes when your heart is full, it leaks out your eyes. I told him of my struggle that morning and my prayer. I bore my testimony that God hears and answers the prayers of mothers. Just as Scott had been nourished by those carrots years ago, so would he be nourished by the word of God. His prayers, too, would be heard and answered.

TOUCHED BY AN ANGEL

One of a woman's greatest assets is the power of a loving touch, and my mother used it to perfection. The warmth of her arms around me, the feel of her soft lips against my cheek, the affectionate squeeze of her hand—none of these sensations could ever be described or duplicated with mere words. As children do, I would sometimes come home in tears over one thing or another, upset that I wasn't chosen to do something at school, that I was left out, or that someone was having a party and I wasn't invited. She never minimized my distress, never dismissed it with, "Oh, that's a silly thing, it's just a little party." My heartbreak was hers; if it brought me to tears, my mother held me and mingled her tears with mine. What's more, as a child, then a teenager, then a grown woman, I never once left or returned home without a kiss from her. After all the years, those kisses are among my most precious memories. I might not recall every word she said, but oh! I do remember the hugs and kisses!

This divine gift of empathy and affection took on new meaning a few years ago when I was in Canada, fulfilling a

Know Your Religion assignment. I spoke at a Relief Society conference that same weekend. After my remarks, a lovely woman came up to me, and beside her was this darling girl who was very, very pregnant. The woman said, "Sister Johnson, I wonder if you would have some words of encouragement for us. This is my daughter. She's nine months pregnant, and the baby has died, and she has had to carry the child, and will have to carry the baby until she goes into labor."

I looked at this dear little face, at this grief-stricken mother standing beside her daughter, and I threw my arms around her and burst into tears. I didn't say a word; all I could do was cry. Later, at our hotel, I wept again in Johnny's arms. I was miserable, and I said to him, "How could I have done that? I feel so stupid. They came to me for encouragement—someone as old and experienced as I, and there were no words. Nothing. I failed them when they needed me most." I was devastated.

The very next day, I received a telephone call at the hotel; it was from this mother. She said, "Sister Johnson, I want you to know that my daughter delivered her dead baby this morning, and we thank you so much for yesterday. We thank you because we felt your empathy and your love and your concern for us. It was more comforting than any words you could have spoken." In that poignant, bittersweet moment, I understood the pure reality of love—the bonding of hearts in mutual understanding and concern. It is the wonderful innate gift and ability of women to feel and express this love in ways that men cannot. If a General Authority of the Church had spoken to this grieving mother and her daughter, perhaps he would have said, "You will always have this child," or some other words of comfort, and his insights would have been appreciated. But it took a woman to truly empathize, to understand what these sisters were feeling, and to literally enfold them in the arms of love. This tender experience taught me an unforgettable lesson—one that my own angel mother had demonstrated time and time again: Words aren't always the things that are needed.

A GOLDEN DECISION

*M*other's perceptive and empathetic heart enabled her to teach me some of life's greatest lessons in the midst of its most turbulent moments. Nearly seventy years ago, as a vulnerable young teenager experiencing the most devastating humiliation and pain I could possibly imagine, I learned from her that sometimes our cruelest misfortunes are really stepping-stones to understanding and compassion.

When I was fourteen, we moved north from southern California to Oakland. It was a terrible time for me; every night I cried myself to sleep because I had no friends in my new school, and I felt that I really didn't belong. Then, after about a month, I was invited by Barbara, the most popular girl in school, to a Halloween party at her home. How thrilled I was! She said it was a costume party, and I should come in the ugliest costume I could find. There would even be a prize given for the ugliest costume. I felt that it was very important for me to follow the party instructions exactly, so I asked Mother to help me dress. I had decided to go as a witch, so we went all out—complete with a pillow in my hunched back, my teeth blackened, and a false hooked nose. I was *really* ugly, and I felt just perfect.

I could hardly contain my excitement as I walked to Barbara's home in one of the richest neighborhoods in town. When I rang the doorbell, her mother came to the door in an evening dress. She gasped when I cackled like a witch and said, "I'm Lucile, and I've been invited to Barbara's Halloween party."

This woman said, with obvious discomfort, "There must be some mistake. This is a best-dress party, and we are having a candlelight dinner." She stood aside and motioned me through the door.

As we entered the elegant dining room, I saw more than a dozen young people, both boys and girls, seated at the formal table in their Sunday best. They all burst into laughter when they saw me. Barbara's mother invited me to sit down, and one of the boys said, "Yes, we have some bat soup for you." Then another said, "Oh, yeah, you'll *love* the fried lizard." All of them roared.

Well, I wouldn't have stayed there if they had offered me a hundred-dollar bill! I don't know how I stumbled out of that house, but I do know what happened next. I burst into tears of humiliation and cried all the way to my home. To this day, I can vividly recall the pain and hurt I felt over such a cruel joke. (And believe me, when my daughters and granddaughters today tell me they feel lonely or ugly or left out, I know *exactly* how they feel.)

When I arrived home, sobbing uncontrollably, my mother took me in her arms, and we sat in her favorite old rocking chair. As I spilled out my story, her own tears splashed down on my face; it was a sweet moment that broke the tension because we laughed together. "I feel your pain," she said, "and I know just how you felt. Let me tell you what happened to me when *I* was fourteen."

Mother told me that when she was my age, she had lived in the country, and the children walked to school. In those days, the girls all wore floor-length dresses, and one morning she and her friends were walking to their little one-room country school. "Lucy Belle," she said, "I don't know quite how it happened, but I stumbled and fell, and my dress came up almost over my head. The kids all laughed so hard they were beside themselves, and I nearly died of humiliation and hurt." When she told me that, we couldn't help laughing at the picture it brought to mind. Then, remembering the pain, we cried a little more. I will never forget her sweet words of comfort, and my heartache was replaced by a feeling of joy and comfort that only a mother can dispense. "You don't believe this now," she whispered, her voice brimming with love, "but I promise you, someday you will come to know that this was a very valuable teaching moment for you."

We talked for more than an hour about how often in life we are called upon to endure humiliation and pain because of someone's cruelty. And Mother was right; this experience taught me more about living the Golden Rule

than I could have learned in any other way. In the wake of my schoolmates' devastating prank, I firmly decided that I must try always to be kind, and never cruel; that it was my responsibility to always be understanding and never unkind to another human being. If I did not do that, I felt it would disappoint the Lord, and it would cause me to eventually become an unpleasant person whom no one would ever want for a friend.

Making this important decision, with my mother's gentle guidance, helped to define my lifelong approach to people, relationships, and circumstances. It also crystallized a principle that I have endeavored to teach my family through the years: A decision, good or bad, once made, becomes the rule of attitude and action from that moment, until recognized and reevaluated if necessary. Life, it seems to me, is a continual process of making decisions, then carefully reviewing and refining them to reflect our most compassionate natures and the deepest strengths of our characters. How grateful I am that my mother's example of unrestrained kindness and generosity toward others enabled me to make the right decision so many years ago. I have come to understand, too, that by relying on our Heavenly Father to help us make the truly important decisions, we can be assured that the choices we make will eventually lead us back to Him. And there will be fewer regrets along the way.

ADVICE TO A BRIDE

*J*ohnny and I met when we were both students at Utah State University, and both of us knew from our very first date that we would marry. Ordinarily, I'm sure Mother wouldn't have been at all pleased to be giving up her darling daughter to a farm boy from Idaho—and a Mormon, no less! But her wise, gentle heart quickly recognized that he was an extraordinarily good, kind man, and she was thrilled that I had found such a decent human being to spend my life with. Because she adored him, I think she was able to overlook the Mormon part.

We were married by an LDS bishop in a lovely ceremony in Santa Rosa, California, on Valentine's Day in 1940. (I did not join the Church until sometime later, after we had moved to Alaska.) That evening, just as the reception was breaking up and we were getting ready to go off on our honeymoon, Mother offered a bit of advice that has influenced my life for over sixty years. "Lucile," she said, and I can still see her blue eyes shining, "it is not Johnny's responsibility to make you happy. The responsibility to be happy lies with you. He can

make you happi*er,* but he is not solely responsible to make you happy. And my darling," she added, "try to be cheerful. I believe that is so important in a marriage. To be cheerful is more important than a pretty face." Through the years, her wise counsel has blessed my life again and again. I truly believe that the decision to be happy and cheerful is a choice we make; no one else is responsible for the happiness we do or do not achieve. I have endeavored to abide by that important principle, and have taught it to my children. *Choosing* happiness is the only way to make sure we have it—and *practicing* it is the only way we can keep it.

Mother might have added that a healthy dose of humor goes a long way toward creating a happy home. I remember that she had the most delicious sense of humor; when I was growing up, she and her three sisters would often get together and tell funny little jokes, laughing over the smallest things, and their wonderful laughing voices would echo all through the house and tickle me until I would be laughing, too. This, of course, was right in the middle of the Great Depression—hard, bitter days when riots were common and people were starving to death—and our lives could well have been weighed down with drudgery and despair. Instead, Mother chose to sprinkle our days liberally with laughter and optimism, illuminating every moment with a certain *joie de vivre* that kept our spirits high. I suspect that at this very moment she is somewhere in the celestial realms enjoying a cozy tête-à-tête with her sisters, sipping hot cocoa and nibbling on small frosted cakes, telling clever little jokes and bringing the heavenly house down!

CARRYING ON

When Mother died suddenly of a massive heart attack at age sixty-seven, none of us were ready to let her go. Yet even in death, she demonstrated her extraordinary ability to bring people together. Although she wasn't a member of the Church, many LDS women knew and loved her, so the Relief Society and the Ladies Aid Society (the Methodist women's auxiliary) joined forces to bid her an affectionate farewell. Her funeral was held in a stake center, complete with loudspeakers outside the building to accommodate the hundreds of people who couldn't be seated inside. Afterward, more lovely people than I could count came up to me and said, "Your mother changed my life. She was so dear and accepting, and she always had time for me. She listened to me, and she said to me, 'You can do it. You just go ahead; you can do that.'" Of course I understood exactly what they were saying, because I, too, had heard those words every day of my life. More than any other individual, she made me feel competent and confident, and she gave me the ability to love people. Even today, as I speak to large groups of women, I look out at them and think, "You wonderful, marvelous sisters," and it often brings me to tears. Then, when they come to me and say, "Sister Johnson, we feel that you really love us," the origin of that precious feeling is reaffirmed in the deepest part of my soul. It came from my beloved mother.

NOT QUITE PERFECT

*I*t has warmed my heart to share with you these sweet, simple memories of growing up under the wing of an extraordinary woman. And I'm quite sure that by now, you picture Maryann Short as a larger-than-life, superhuman model of perfect motherhood. Indeed, I am often tempted to remember her that way myself, and with good reason. Mother was one of the kindest, most loving, generous-natured, and nonjudgmental women on the planet. I don't recall ever hearing her gossip or speak unkindly about another human being, and I can never remember when she disciplined me or was harsh or critical or lost her temper or raised her voice. But the fact is, I'm sure she did *all* of those things at one time or another—as any mother would (and let me tell you, my brother and I were not by any means model children!). Maryann Short was not perfect; only the Lord Jesus Christ can claim that accomplishment. But Mother loved her family perfectly; so in the end, little else mattered. Of course there must have been incidents of anger and chastisement and frustration and disappointment; these are all necessary, inescapable parts of our mortal experience. But the moments of deep, genuine love outnumbered them so profusely that I honestly can't remember even one of them. That, I believe, is one of the greatest keys to being a successful mother: loving one's children without condition or reservation, and making sure they know it and feel it every single day of their lives. I learned this great truth from my mother; it has been passed down to my own children and shared with thousands of beautiful sisters whom I have met through the years.

And now, in honor of the woman whose daily devotion to her family made all the difference, I would like to relate a few of my own observations about mothers and their singular role in Heavenly Father's plan.

LESSONS FOR LIFE

I firmly believe that there has never been a time in history that has been more difficult or challenging for women than this very day. As the adversary increases his relentless assault on the family, Latter-day Saint mothers and other righteous women are called upon to rear the most elect generation of God's spirit children. It's all-out war—but there's no doubt in my mind that you mothers of Zion are up to it! It's true that times are different from what they were in my day; circumstances are different; the world is changing more rapidly than we can even comprehend. In fact, some of you younger women might feel that there is so much of a "generation gap" between us that anything I might say simply wouldn't be relevant to your lives. However, please remember that while times and toys and technologies change, pretty much everything else remains the same. The situations and experiences that bring us pain and hurt and anxiety today, that cause us to feel burdened with stress and isolation, are exactly the same things that caused me to feel that way eighty years

ago. My feelings of inadequacy and loneliness and heartache as a young wife and mother were the same as what you are feeling today. By the same token, the basic good and noble things in life—love, faith, acceptance, kindness, the willingness to stretch and grow, to risk ourselves, to help others—never lose their power to bless and elevate and refine our spirits. So you see, there isn't much that separates us after all.

My counsel to all mothers is time-tested and straightforward: Every child in your life needs and deserves abundant and unqualified love, loyalty, acceptance, and feelings of safety. If these qualities are present in your home, you will be fulfilling your divine calling. It simply doesn't matter how big your bank account is, what educational degrees you hold, how expert you are on the Internet, or what neighborhood you call home.

A number of years ago, I was asked to appear in court with a young boy, a member of the Church, who had done some inappropriate things and was considered a juvenile delinquent. As I visited with his distraught mother, she said, "You know, Lucile, I can't understand how this has happened. I've done everything for my son; I've kept an immaculate home, made sure he always had clean, neat clothes, cooked him wonderful meals. But now he's just gone off the deep end." She shook her head in disbelief and despair.

I, too, shook my head, but it was for a different reason. "I want to tell you something," I said. "I promise you that no child is ever going to grow up believing how much you loved him because his drawer was full of clean underwear. That is no indicator to a child that his mother loves him. He will probably never even remember the great suppers you prepared for him. But you know what? Later on, when he's older, he'll always remember the times when you put your arms around him and kissed him. He'll remember the feeling, and he'll remember that you loved him." I could see by the look in this mother's eyes that I had given her something to think about.

We can always do better. A sweet mother named Isabel shared this experience with me: "I have a boy who helps me with the dishes, and that has been wonderful. He had always been especially careful with my mother's fine china, but the day of testing inevitably came. One Thanksgiving when he was about eleven, I gave him a big turkey platter to carry . . . something happened and it slipped from his grasp, shattering into little pieces on the floor. The color drained from my son's face, and his expression filled with horror to see what he had done.

"By all rights, I should have been furious. But at that moment, somewhere inside of me, the Spirit gave me these words: 'Robbie, how many times have you wiped dishes for me? Maybe you have done it dozens of times, and you have never, ever broken a dish. So I think it's owed. Today, it's all right for you to break a dish.' I looked at my son's face, flooded with disbelief when he heard me say that. Then I just threw my arms around him and gave him a big kiss."

Through my tears, I said to her, "Isabel, as long as your boy lives, he will never forget that he broke his mother's best turkey platter. If you had said, 'You idiot! Look what you've done! My set's ruined!', it would have been a painful and bitter memory. But instead, he'll always remember your words of love."

I share this experience because I believe it illustrates a vital ingredient in any mother's recipe for success: the influence of the Spirit. As women, we are entitled to this divine gift; nothing can impact or empower us more. We can ask for it in our daily prayers, learn to recognize its promptings, and call upon it to replace anger with loving patience, melt frustration into calm forbearance, turn indecision into purpose and direction, and compensate for a great many of our other human frailties. Like a prism of heavenly light, it magnifies our love for others and enables us to maintain a home where our children can feel safe and at peace. This is truly one of the "best gifts" promised by the Lord if we seek them (see D&C 46:8), and I believe that He is deeply pleased when we ask for the Spirit's benevolent and protective influence as we nurture our families.

When I was a young wife and mother, often separated from my husband for months or even years at a time because of his military assignments, I developed a habit of rising early in the morning, before anyone else was up, and immersing myself in quiet contemplation, scripture study, and fervent prayer in behalf of myself and my family. I pleaded with the Lord to grant me patience, a cheerful and loving heart, inspiration to deal with the events of the day, the right words to say, and the faith and courage to be the best mother I could possibly be. Looking back on all of those years and all of those prayers, I believe the blessings came because I was willing to ask for them. Heavenly Father knows that the love of a mother for her child perhaps comes as close to divine love as a human being is capable of, and He stands ready to help you express that love in ways that will bless your family forever. Just ask!

I believe that women today have greater responsibilities and challenges because more of them are employed outside the home. This is a consequence of modern-day economics; I do not believe that most working Latter-day Saint women have jobs because they want to buy a mink coat or pay for a Mercedes. In reality, they're out in the workplace because, finances being what they are, they need to help pay for the mortgage and for other necessities of life. Their hearts are in the right place. I speak to so many LDS mothers who have said, "Lucile, I would give anything in the world if I had the luxury to stay home with my children." To you dear sisters, I would say that you have a tremendous responsibility to make mothering your priority, even though you can't be in the home as much as you'd like.

The scenario can be staggering. By the time you get home after a long day at work, most of your energy has been spent in the marketplace, you're bone-tired, and there's still a meal to be prepared, cleaning to be done, and homework to be supervised. It's a great temptation to toss a frozen dinner into the microwave, then spend the rest of the evening being cross or impatient or distracted, even ignoring your children. But whenever these temptations come, remember the power of inviting the Spirit into your home and your heart. These hours with your family are precious and few; use them wisely to shower your children with love, to throw your arms around them, to read to them, to laugh and cry and play and dream with them. In the eternal scheme of things, nothing else really matters. You can do it; Heavenly Father will help! Remember: they're His children, too.

A FEW FINAL THOUGHTS

*M*any years have passed since that little straight-haired, toothless Lucile Short somehow managed to capture the "Better Baby Contest" prize. Now I watch in awe as my own children, grandchildren, and great-grandchildren accomplish amazing things every day of their lives. As I see their futures unfolding, I am continually reminded of the precious woman who gave so freely of herself, who loved her children so abundantly and provided a safe haven for them, and whose brilliant legacy will be passed on for many generations to come. I see my mother in the shining eyes and contagious smiles at every family gathering, and I realize that for me to be truly, truly happy, she would have to be a part of my eternal life. This, I believe, is why a loving Father saw fit to provide me with such a powerful confirmation of Mother's acceptance of the gospel and its sacred temple ordinances. I simply cannot imagine a celestial life without her.

Helen Keller once observed, "With the death of every friend I love, a part of me has been buried. But their contri-

bution to my being, to my happiness, strength, and understanding remains to sustain me in an altered world." This is exactly what has happened to me since the extraordinary woman who gave me life was called home, far too soon, at the age of sixty-seven—she has reached beyond the veil to sustain and strengthen me every step of the way. I can only hope and pray that somewhere along the well-traveled road, her precious Lucy Belle has done a few things to bring a smile to her lovely face.

One day (and at my age, it's likely to be sooner than later), I will see my beloved mother again. When that transcendent moment arrives, I will drop to my knees, throw my arms around her, and say, "Thank you, Mother, thank you, thank you for preparing me so well for my sojourn on earth." Even if I had been born under the gospel covenant, she could not have gifted me more than she did, for her boundless love opened my heart to endless possibilities—including the tender whisperings of the Spirit and my eventual conversion to the Church. Now that we are all numbered safely among the Good Shepherd's flock, I look forward with great joy to feeling her arms around me once again, smelling the sweet fragrance of her. With Mother beside me, there will be no need to ask where I am. It will be heaven.

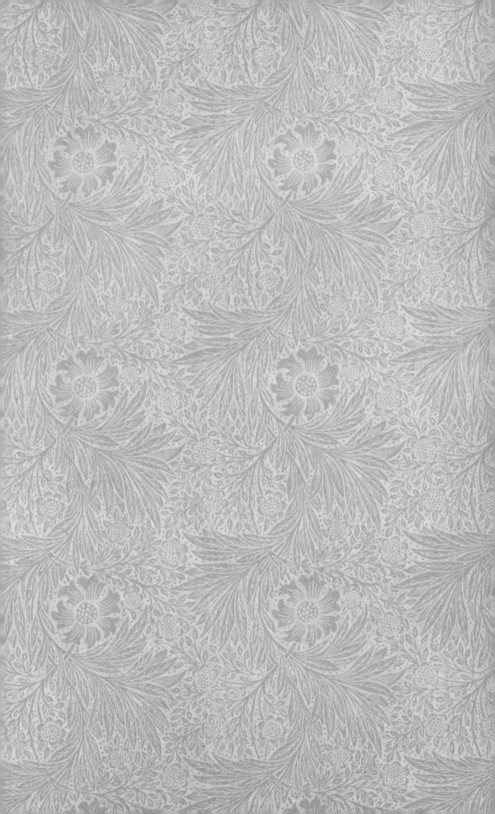